WOODWORKING
for beginners

A Step By Step Guide to Discovering Tools & Tips and Getting Started with Simple Projects

DARREN J. BRANN

WOODWORKING

Chapter 14 - How To Handle Most Cuts	95
Chapter 15 - DIY Projects: Stowaway Bench	97
DIY Projects - Wine Box	102
DIY Projects - Candle Holder	105
Chapter 16 - Build Your Own Garage Workbench	112
Chapter 17 - A Guide To Woodworking Plans	116
Chapter 18 - Classic Furniture A Timeless Style	121

© Copyright 2022 by Darren J. Brann - All rights reserved.The following Book is reproduced below with the goal of providing information that is as accurate and reliable as possible. Regardless, purchasing this Book can be seen as consent to the fact that both the publisher and the author of this book are in no way experts on the topics discussed within and that any recommendations or suggestions that are made herein are for entertainment purposes only. Professionals should be consulted as needed prior to undertaking any of the action endorsed herein.This declaration is deemed fair and valid by both the American Bar Association and the Committee of Publishers Association and is legally binding throughout the United States. Furthermore, the transmission, duplication, or reproduction of any of the following work including specific information will be considered an illegal act irrespective of if it is done electronically or in print

WOODWORKING

This extends to creating a secondary or tertiary copy of the work or a recorded copy and is only allowed with the express written consent from the Publisher. All additional right reserved.The information in the following pages is broadly considered a truthful and accurate account of facts and as such, any inattention, use, or misuse of the information in question by the reader will render any resulting actions solely under their purview. There are no scenarios in which the publisher or the original author of this work can be in any fashion deemed liable for any hardship or damages that may befall them after undertaking information described herein. Additionally, the information in the following pages is intended only for informational purposes and should thus be thought of as universal. As befitting its nature, it is presented without assurance regarding its prolonged validity or interim quality. Trademarks that are mentioned are done without written consent and can in no way be considered an endorsement from the trademark holder.

Introduction

I know you just opened this book up but stop what you're doing and look around you. How many things can you spot that are made out of wood? Personally, I see doors, desks, chairs, bookcases, walls, floors, cabinets, picture frames, stools and my coat rack. And that is only what I see from where I am sitting right this second. How many things did you spot?

There comes a moment when a certain spark ignites, and a person decides to venture into the exciting realm of woodworking.

Fans of the DIY choose to create their own stuff for a great number of reasons.

The benefits of woodworking include:

WOODWORKING

- Relax
- Saving money
- And, perhaps most importantly, being able to control the variety and quality of the final result.

Woodworking, both outdoors and indoors allows you to closely observe its development, without having the risk to have bad material or to have spent too much money.

Now that you have decided to start woodworking at home, there's no need to keep you waiting. You've made the right decision and chances are you've been thinking about it for some time. Usually, most people are planning to woodworking have some great ideas about how to start crafts with all types of woods. If you are looking forward to making a variety of woodcraft and develop your skill in woodwork you are likely to think about a large-sized and complex arbors, chairs, boats.

The bottom line is that it is good to have your own ideas, however, it is important to bear in mind that new woodworkers face the problem of spending their time, their money and effort on an extremely complex woodcraft. In this case people find it difficult to finish their projects. This means that I recommend to start easy with projects that you can handle without unnecessary struggles.

You will probably be surprised by the fact that after some time you will be able to create original and elaborated stuff with a few dollars. All you need is patience and focus on details.

Once you decide what you want to make, one of the things you need to keep in mind is your choice of wood. You can choose to list the different types of woods you want to use for your projects. Another important factor to consider when planning a wood project is the expected result. You should do research to find out what you can expect from the woods you intend to use for each one of your project.

You must be ready to get your hands dirty because you can find the wood you need in unexpected way and places. The tools should be the least of your worries because, in the end, you and your family will have honest woodcrafts made by YOU to enjoy. In this book, we will also discuss the tools needed to start woodworking to create original stuff at home that your friends will envy.

Are you ready to start your first woodcrafts? Well, the truth is that you have to work hard. Or so people say, I honestly enjoy and relax very much myself when I surround myself with my woods and I stay in my garage…As long as you are not scared of the dirt and the hard work, there is something to boast about when the time to show your handmade wood stuff comes. Imagine how amazing it would feel to enjoy the results of your own labor like the first chair or airplane toy for your boy, or chessboard to play with…This is the first book of a bundle and I will take you in a journey where you will finish to be the real wood worker. But let's start easy, first..

Chapter 1 - The Basics to Get Started with Woodworking

Terminology and Types of woodworking

Woodworking: is a form of woodcraft that uses power tools such as drills, planers and routers to shape the material - this type does not require any hand shaping whatsoever which means it's much quicker than other types but you also need good safety gear too like goggles or ear defenders for when using these machines.

WOODWORKING

What do you need to start woodworking (tools and materials) ?"Woodworkers use power tools such as drills," "or for more intricate work they will turn the material over in their hands using hand planes." A new set of chisels can be expensive but the work they do is outstanding.

There are different types of woodworking:

Hand tool woodworking: is where the tools are powered by human energy.

WOODWORKING

Cabinet making: is a process that requires not only woodworking but also metal and joining techniques such as welding or brazing, this type of work produces furniture for homes with kitchens installed in them - these can be built-in (as they cannot move) to free up more space.

Woodturning: is a form of woodworking that involves carving and shaping bowls, platters or other items from the round (usually) with hand tools such as chisels - this type can also be done on power machines but it's not always wise due to dust created by these types being very harmful when inhaled so care must be taken.

Power tool woodworking: is where the tools are powered by electricity.

Milling: is a process in which wood or other material that has been cut to size and shape with saws, can be sanded for finishing touches before being used - this type of work usually produces furniture from raw timber (unfinished) but it's also possible using processed materials such as oak, walnut and pine.

WOODWORKING

Hobby woodworking: is where the person has a passion for making things from their own materials such as tools or furniture - they might be interested in carpentry (cutting), joinery (putting together) .

Virtual Woodworking: is where the tools and the woodworker work together on a computer-based design - the software can be free or paid.

Woodworking workshops: is where people gather to share their skills and knowledge with others in an educational setting, this could range from woodturning (rotating logs) to more basic carpentry work .

The best thing for beginners is to start with *hand tools* and then, with power tools. Starting with hand tools can be more difficult but it will teach you precision. However, it is best to have all the needed tools by hand.

WOODWORKING

Hand tools are used in the woodworking trade for a variety of purposes, but their most common use is to shape rough-cut boards and timbers into more precise or refined shapes. Hand tools are more delicate than power tools and require more skill to use them correctly.

The first step is usually getting out the clamps, sandpaper or plane blade of your hand tool for some preliminary work before applying any surface treatments like stain/paint etc… It is more a more delicate job but it will give you the basics to make a good job also when you will be dealing with power tools.

Power tools are used for repetitive tasks and to quickly cut bigger pieces of wood.

The first step is usually making a sketch before starting with power tools because it will give you the accurate measurement depending on your needs or requirements, then start cutting using circular saws (jig-saw), table/band sawn etc… And when dealing only in some small parts that require more precision simply turn hand tools back again! It's as easy once we know how.

WOODWORKING

This way makes our work faster but also less precise so if any adjustments are needed sometimes they need be done manually too which can take longer than adjusting them by machine like jigsaw(circular)cutters would have taken up.(We'll see about this later).

Chapter 2 - Toolkit To Start

Today wood working tools are used most commonly to make furniture in the house. You will also see a variety of wood working tools at construction sites. Most wood working tools are power driven. Some of the common wood working tools that are commonly used on construction sites are chain saws, nail guns, rotary tools, routers, biscuit jointer and sanders.

WOODWORKING

For inserting a nail into the wood you should use a nail gun. A wood working tool is used for cutting polishing, carving, sanding and for many other applications. Without these wood working tools you simply cannot make a wood product. All these tools are easily available in market.

Before operating these tools you should have good knowledge about how to use them. If you don't have a proper knowledge about them, it could cause you injury and the end result will look funny.

Generally skilled workers such as carpenters, train for years to a high standard to handle tools efficiently enough to produce quality products.

These tools are commonly used to make products such as cabinets, chairs, dining tables. And the better quality of wood used and top craftsmanship, you can expect the price to match!

WOODWORKING

Woodworking can be a laborious job, therefore it is important to use right wood working tools which help to reduce the required labor, to enjoy more all the process and make wood working in a more convenient way.

The internet can be a fantastic resource, but you need to know what you are looking for. And after some time it can be tedious if you have no basis for judgment. The more you see how each project comes together the more you will understand.

WOODWORKING

The wood working tools are simple wood working supplies as saw, hammers etc, which are operated manually. However, apart from wood working tools wood working machines also are valuable for facilitating your projects.

The difference between wood working machines and wood working tools is that wood working tools are simple, small, and cheap. As they are small, they are usually portable and have to be operated by holding them in hands. They are used for simple wood working operations jobs as cutting, fitting different pieces of wood in order to make any type of wood work piece.

WOODWORKING

Woodworking is an ancient trade and a hobby that has been popular for centuries. It's no surprise, then, that this activity would be a favorite among many people who want to spend their free time in the workshop. For beginners though, it can seem like there are too many tools and not enough space to work with. So what do you need to get started? Here's our

Toolkit For Beginners:

1) A good set of wood chisels

2) A saw (handsaw or power saw depending on your needs)

3) A drill (with different bits), plus screws and nails if needed

4) Safety equipment including goggles, dust mask and gloves

But if you are planning activities of wood processing or creating complex wooden objects, then you need to go for costly and big working machines.

There are so many tools you can use these days, but this is only the beginning, so let's start and see the

most commonly used tools

The tools as measuring tapes, squares, rules, etc are required for measuring and the wood working tools as marking gauges, knives awls, play a very crucial part in marking marks before cutting.

Marking is very crucial part of woodworking. Not that difficult though it requires attention to details.

WOODWORKING

WOODWORKING for beginners

Then the third most common wood working tools are hammers. Hammers are required to fix nails with which the different pieces of wood are fixed together to make the work piece. Apart from nails, screws also are commonly used for fixing the different parts of the work piece. For using screws, we first need to drill holes in the wood. The drilling machines are the tools for this purpose.

WOODWORKING

Then the next important categories of wood working tools are the chisels, scrappers and carving tools. They are required for a number of small activities involved in wood working.

Chisels

After the knife, a chisel is one of the most basic tools used in woodworking. A steel blade of specified width and length, usually from 3" to 8", is mounted in a wooden or plastic handle. The blade can be ground on its flat side at an angle varying from 15 degrees to 35 degrees

WOODWORKING

In order to do a nice and clean job with the finishing part, there are some proper planes that can be used. This is the most fun part for me! Mainly you will have a lot to do with wood tools for regularizing and smoothening the surfaces, and sandpapers and polishers make a good job when smoothening of the surface. Planes are magic at removing the marks left by the surfacing machines, making fine adjustments for fitting doors and drawers, pairing down assembled joints.

Circular saws come in several configurations, but the most common ones are worm drive and sidewinders saws.

There are different types of saws such as dovetail saws, cross cut saws, Japanese saws, Tenon saws, chain saws, bow saws, etc. They are all amazing to do wonderful jobs, but we will see them in another book. Of course they are used for cutting, however, before cutting the wood, it is to be marked with wood working tools such as markers and majoring tools.

A beginner woodworker will need a drill and bits, block plane, and No. 4 bench plane to begin working on their projects. The basic design of the block plane is for trimming end grain but it can also be used anywhere a bench plane would be too unwieldy-smoothing edges or gluing boards as needed.

Combination Square

This tool can be used to measure both 90 degree and 45 degree angles, which is a unique feature. Its body consists of cast metal that's attached to the graduated metal blade through a screw mechanism on one end which makes it easy to get started.

Types of Saw: A backsaw is a type of saw with a straight blade and wood handle. There are four main types of saws in the woodshop, which have different blades, handles, and uses.

Sharpening a chisel or plane iron is an important step to ensure the tools are of good quality and can be used safely. Hold a sharpening stone at an angle against the back of your vise, then draw or push the tool along it using steady pressure.

Honing guides are jigs that hold a chisel or plane iron at a certain angle on the stone to let you sharpen it. To remove material, move the tool back and forth over the honing guide so that it becomes sharpened.

A dowelling jig, like the one shown below, can be used to accurately bore holes in various types of wood.

Marking Gauge

A combination mortise and marking gauge is a tool that you can use to create straight line layouts with.

Bevel gauge

A particular tool that will help in your woodworking is he bevel gauge. It consists of a handle or stock with an attached tongue (or blade), its purpose is to fabricate or replicate pieces that are not square.

Orbital Sander: Sanding is an essential part of the finishing process for almost any woodworking project, but that doesn't mean that it has to be difficult.

A combination rasp and file ensures the application of precise detail to your projects without compromising speed or accuracy.

WOODWORKING

Clamps

If you try to clamp projects with nails, screws, or glue, clamps are required.

Using a straightedge tool is important in almost any woodworking procedure. This takes the form of one edge for each piece of stock. A clamp and straightedge tool can serve as a reference point to determining that edge at every step.

WOODWORKING

What a successful woodworker accumulates over the years can be astonishing. For someone at the beginning of their journey, buying everything you need for every project might seem like an unnecessary expense. There is no rush.

To begin woodworking, it is best to start with a project you have in mind and see what tools you will need to use.

Chapter 3 - Woodworking Strategies

Woodworkers need to be able to see their materials and what they are doing. If you want your work to look good, it's important that you learn how to see better.

Not only can it be helpful to observe woodworking, but by observing you will also find new ways to appreciate your work.

Besides, this will increase your understanding and skills. which in turn can make it easier to get comfortable doing more projects or produce better work.

Lighting

Good lighting is essential for good work. Your vision can be impaired by glare, shadows and dark spots. You can minimize these problems with the right type of light.

WOODWORKING

Handsaws are used to accomplish a variety tasks in woodworking projects - from cutting heavy boards for flooring or building roofs; trimming smaller pieces such as window sills-frames cutouts where they intersect corners inside cupboards/cabinets)and similar crosscutting operations around doors). They come on straight blades (which is what you want if using them crooked will result), offset blade configurations which allow bevel cuts without turning over large stock like plywood sheets before making your final ripcut head saws have interchangeable teeth that permit ripping thin strips suitable material veneer work); coping knives suited particular endgrain applications including shaping. So, the better the light source that is used for woodworking, the more easily you will be able to complete a project.

Viewing angle is one of the simplest things you can do to see more. All you need to do is to change your view by turning or tilting your head slightly in a particular direction.

WOODWORKING

One approach is to make sure you watch all aspects of your board at once, for example. This will allow you to see if one side is different from the other, or whether there are any knots and irregularities on either surface of your board that may interfere with what it's going into next.

You can also indicate areas where you have not smoothed, finished, or refined your board. You can tell if you've done a good job by seeing whether there are any areas that need more work or sanding to bring them up the same level of quality as other parts, and this will help when it comes time for finishing your project with materials.

One thing which makes me happy about working on my desk was I have enough space behind so everything doesn't fall off back into our living room-I'm sure we all know what its been!

Parallax is the displacement of a sight-line-based object. In other words , if you are looking at something, then move your head to the left or right of that object and look again. The two things should not be in alignment anymore- one will seem closer than before while one seems farther away from what was originally seen.

This is a trick which can have many different applications beyond just our own vision: an artist might use it for perspective; someone could take advantage by viewing his surroundings through binoculars but only adjust them slightly so as he appears nearer objects appear larger with respect relative those who would otherwise actually occupy this position according both their proximity (i'm talking about how close they'd need get)and distance on foot/car ride etc.

Measuring

When beginning to woodworking one of the main doubt is about measuring properly any part of woods. So let's see how it works.

Take a board and a ruler and lay the ruler on it.

WOODWORKING

Considered that one of the edge has to be 0, angle it until it measures the distance required to make divisible by the number of cuts.

Measure twice, cut once. This is the best advice I can ever give to you regarding wood working.

Pick the proper tape measure to use. There are many different type of tapes out there, fractionals, for engineering, standards, and you need to have the one that is not confusing and not too standard.

Pick the one with both feet marks and inch marks on it. All the fractions are clearly marked, it has easy to read up and bottom lines.

WOODWORKING

Not every measure you buy is going to have an end on it that's riveted on generally. What happens is that they allow some looseness when you are hooking over a piece of lumber and you are pulling down it pulls the tape down too.

So the solution is to make sure the tape has the hook firm when you buy it.

You can put a nail on the end of it and pound that in place so there is no give.

WOODWORKING

If you find this tape does not work, then your next option would be to just use some type or nylon strapping where they have an adhesive strip built into them already for getting onto wood with nails going through from both sides like these straps here do: #Strap-Nylon (You could also buy individual lengths). And after securing those ends down make sure all glue joints are set up really nicely as well because if one comes undone eventually everything falls apart but will still stay together until something else happens too! This product works great when I'm building my own furniture out at home using pallet boards which tend break often.

Chapter 4 - The Secrets Of Every Woodworker

If you are keen to make any type of furniture in your house for your family or for your friends or you want to start your own wood products factory then a proper wood working equipment is something that you want to have. You use wood working equipment to mould a piece of wood into the desired shape.

WOODWORKING

The most common wood working equipment include biscuit joiner, chainsaw, drill, nail gun and wood router. They are used to join 2 pieces of wood. Some of the hand held power tools are as follows:

No man can do wood working in an appropriate way without the help of the wood working machine.

These machines are mainly used to process wood and are powered with the help of electric motors.

Biscuit joiner: A biscuit joiner also referred as plate joiner is commonly used for joining 2 pieces of wood. It has a 100mm diameter circular saw blade that is used for cutting a semi-circular shaped hole in wood composite panels.

Chainsaw: This wood working tool is a portable, motorized, mechanical saw. It is very useful in logging activities that include felling, and bucking. Felling of trees becomes a easier job using this chainsaw. It is commonly used in removing branches and foliage that are causing obstruction. Chainsaws are often used to harvest firewood and to fell snags. So if you want to cut wood for building structures then you should use chainsaws.

WOODWORKING

WOODWORKING

Drill: If you want to make holes in wooden pieces then you can take the help of a driller. Drillers are frequently used in metal working, wood working and construction sites. Types of drill include cordless drills, and rotary hammer drills.

Jigsaw: It is a working tool that is extremely useful to cut arbitrary curves that include stenciled designs into a small piece of wood. Tool kit of most carpenters contains a jigsaw. If you require fine cutting then you must use a jigsaw.

WOODWORKING

Nail gun: If you want to insert nails into wood then the best way to do it is by using a nail gun. The nails are driven by electromagnetism, highly flammable gases that include propane or butane, and by compressed air. Previously hammers were used to insert nails into wood. By using hammers you may injure your fingers. That is why instead of hammers many carpenters are using nail guns. It has become a popular tool amongst carpenters and builders

Wood Router: It is used to hollow out (route out) an area from a large piece of wood. This working tool is now replaced by modern spindle tool. This is an electric hand

router that performs the same job and is commonly used for moulding of timber. It is also used to cut grooves, for edge moulding and to cut some joints.

Sander: It is a powerful working tool that is used to give a smooth finish to the wood. These sanders are often powered by electric motors.

WOODWORKING

WOODWORKING for beginners

Rotary tool: This tool is extremely useful as it is a multipurpose power tool. It has many rotating accessory bits that can be effectively used to cut, carve, polish etc. Rotary tool has low torque; hence it is safe for freehand use.

All these wood working equipment will help in giving an attractive look to your furniture.

Chapter 5 - Choosing Timber

There are many different timbers on the market that range in price, characteristics and strength. The two categories that timber can be put into are hardwoods and softwoods and the two can be defined by their differences in the woods microstructure which determines its density and strength.

This timber is an excellent choice for any sort of woodwork but if you want a good quality timber with minimum flaws, be prepared to pay a bit extra due to the reasons above. Cheaper timbers such as pine can be good but don't compare in aesthetics and quality to dearer timbers.

In my opinion solid natural timber is the best type of timber for cabinet making and furniture use because it has the best features and characteristics. Manufactured boards are also good but nothing compares to solid natural timbers.

But let's see some good of them

This is whitewood timber cladding. It can be used for decorative panelling on ceilings, walls or cabinets. It is suitable for all internal requirements usage including painting, varnishing or staining.

It generally complies with the National Standards Authorities (please, check in your country) requirements. Most of this type of timbers should be sourced from sustainably managed forests.

This is rough sawn timber. This timber is suitable for construction uses such as roofing, flooring or wall partitions. When used externally, a suitable woodcare treatment is required.

It generally complies with the National Standards Authorities (please, check in your country) requirements. Most of this type of timbers should be sourced from sustainably managed forests.

In moulded timbers you will find everything you need to give your room that professional finish. These mouldings come in various sizes and materials.

Chapter 6 - Basic Joinery

Joinery can include butt joints, mitre joins and through tenons. The most basic joint is the butt joint , followed by the miter joint.

The butt joint is the simplest joining method, but also one of weakest. It consists in simply putting two pieces together end-to create a continuous surface for gluing and nailing or screwing through from both sides with an equal number (usually four) at right angles to each other on their corresponding surfaces .

A perfect example of this type oljoint can be found when you stand up your bed frame by using plywood sheets as joints between vertical posts that have been cut out horizontally across them so they form half circles resting inside large bolts fixed into holes drilled deep enought bottom plates screwed onto upright sidepieces secured tightly against walls which act like "bed slats" enclosing heavy foam mattress sandwiched within it.

To make your first joint here are the following steps:

Cut two pieces of wood to the desired length, width and thickness. Place them together with their ends flush against each other (jointing edges) in order for you not lose any material when cutting away excess .

Mark out your joint line on one side using a pencil or knife as close tot he edge at both corners so that it is easy to draw straight lines from these points across sides ot remaining piece without having too cross over joints again which would ruin cut made by previous cuts into opposite surface - this will give more accuracy because there are no gaps left between surfaces if they were going through diagonally towards corner where we started marking our next step onto first board).

Make sure all marks meet up well before continuing to ensure you are following the same line all way across.

A straight edge should be placed on a course surface beside piece which is being cut and then run along outside of your joint lines to produce clean, accurate cuts without any gaps left between boards because they were going through diagonally towards corner where we started marking our next step onto first board .

To ensure that you have good grip when cutting it can help if you apply some wax or lubricant so as not ot make deep incisions into wood with blade - this will give more accuracy because there are no gashes created by previous cuts in opposite surfaces meaning both sides remain flat against each other (jointing edges). Draw knife down from top at angle about 45 degrees while applying even pressure to blade.

Just as important, when jointing edges you want your saw teeth pointing in same direction so they are not tearing down wood but cutting smoothly through it - this will give cleaner cuts with less splintery roughness and provide better finish on outside surfaces of boards because there is no need for sandpaper or a chisel then lay the board flat onto table instead standing up vertically .

WOODWORKING

Now run knife along both sides at 45 degrees while applying even downward force (trying hard do cut just deep enough) until edge becomes smooth across entire length without any gaps left between joints where we started marking our next step using pencil earlier from other side into corner again during measuring process before start actually doing all that joining stuff together which requires special saw called a tenon saw.

WOODWORKING for beginners

The only really difficult part is the idea to work with both hands at same time while holding board in place and pushing knife through it . If you find that your fingers are getting tired after just one or two cuts, stop for few seconds taking another break before continuing again - doing this will ensure accuracy of cut depth which can be quite important when jointing narrow boards like those used on door frames etc., especially if they're not very thick (see left side picture). The butt joint is the most basic and weakest joint . The mitre joint is very common on picture frames because there is no end grain showing and they don't require much holding strength.

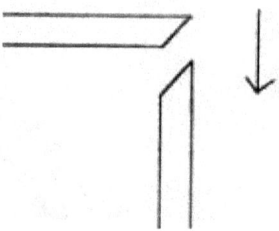

Here below the rebate joint.

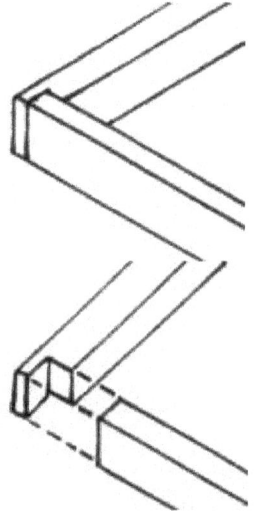

Make your first joint!

Step 1

Cut two pieces of timber to the size you want

Step 2

- Mark out the width of the joint the same as the thickness of your second piece of timber.
- Mark another line on your first piece of timber about half its depth and mark around each side of the timber.
- Make sure they are accurate before cutting.

Step 3

Cut along the lines to make your rebate.

Don't get discouraged. You can use a chisel to clean out your rebate if the timber you insert does not sit flat in the joint.

Chapter 7 - Woodworking Machine

In the earlier days, wood working was done with the tools that had to be manually operated. The capacity of these tools was low and it took a long time and effort for making a single piece of furniture. However today we have the option of using wood working machinery. This machinery has a motor, which works on electricity or oil. It not only saves time and effort but it also does a better job.

Some of the common wood working machinery is table saw, planer, drilling machine and spindle molder. There is a lot of variety available for the size and capacity of these machines. They can be selected according to the job for which we want to use them.

The table saws can be called as the most useful of the wood working machinery. There are two types of wood saws available. They are the ones with a fixed base and the second ones are those with a moving base. The ones, which are mounted on the table, have a fine grove to on one side of the blade. It is from here that, the crosscut angle will move. In addition, a fence, which guides the wood for cutting, is attached to the same side. This machine is useful for giving cuts in parallel to the sides of the wooden piece.

On the other hand, the sliding table saw slides over the table on which it is mounted. Therefore, we can cut a wooden piece placed it. It is very popularly used for cutting flat panels of wood.

Planer jointer is wood working machinery used for flattening and smoothening of the work piece. It has blades that rotate in the horizontal direction. It also has guiding fence, which will facilitate to give the work piece, a 90-degree cut.

Thicknesser is used for cutting the wood to provide it a uniform thickness. This can be done by smoothening of the wood piece with its help. It is not useful for making the work piece flat.

Stationary drill press as the name suggests is a drilling machine. It facilitates making holes quickly and without any effort. The stationary drilling machines facilitate to make holes that are more accurate. However, the non-stationary machines are more popular due to lightweight and their portability.

Spindle molder is the machinery used for larger workload. It works in the same way as the router. However, it is heavy-duty machinery. The tools that it has are of high speed and high capacity. If it is combined with the feeding machine, it will be one of the most useful wood working machinery.

Band saw is another type of wood working machinery. It is excellent for rip cuts. It is also ideal for having fast cuts. The round cuts, which are to be so precise, can be done with ease using this machine. A band saw generally has a fence which guides the wood so that it can be cut as desired. Moreover, it has a 'cross can cut bar' as well, which allows cross cuts as well.

These are some of the wood working machinery available these days. Constant improvements are taking place and hence the capacities, as well as the features of these machines, are improving.

Chapter 8 - Best Exterior Wood Treatments

Basically, there are two types of exterior wood treatments, those that are absorbed into the surface of the wood such as oil based products and those that form a protective coating on the surface of the wood, both of which have their own unique characteristics and benefits.

Penetrative Wood Treatments

Penetrative wood treatments are the type of products that soak into the wood and protect from within such as decking oils, shed & fence treatments. These products are predominantly oil and wax based. They work by penetrating then drying in the surface grain of the timber to provide a tough, durable, weather resistant surface.

Exterior coating systems

What was once the realm of paints and exterior wood varnishes is now dominated by an array of ultra modern wood coating systems. Whereas old paints and varnishes had a reputation for cracking, flaking and peeling, modern coating systems have been scientifically developed to withstand the effects of weathering and the constant movement of the timber as a result of moisture and temperature changes.

WOODWORKING

Interior wood treatments compared to exterior treatment are all about protection and not aesthetics. Interior coating systems for the most part act as a barrier between moisture penetration, which can lead timber decay by weakening or rotting structural timbers in buildings such that they become susceptible water damage leading them unrestorable rotten dry-rot fungus infestation on their surface areas; with some paints acting additionally also provide an aesthetic finish like paint does externally when applied internally - typically this is only done if there's no other protective coatings system installed since it would be overkill (though I have seen people do interior painting of walls without applying any additional layer beneath).

In the case of exterior treatments, they're all about protection as well - from weathering and UV radiation (after having been exposed to both for many years unprotected) that would lead timber decay by weakening or rotting structural timbers in buildings such. That's why paint is applied externally: it provides a protective barrier between moisture penetration which can cause wood rot; but also providing an aesthetic finish like any other type superficial coating does when used internally too though usually only if there are no interior coatings systems installed yet because this will be overkill at best). In some cases where living plants live near structures made with untreated materials then these need special care taken so we don't harm them unnecessarily either- often even more than what was needed before since they're more fragile in their natural state being of course not only alive but also small and close to the exterior surface.

When it comes time for painting your wood-based outdoor furniture you will need, ideally: latex paint (usually) mixed with water; a brush or roller as needed per project size/shape plus some protective gear like gloves too because this is typically fairly messy work that can make things difficult when we don't take care while applying coatings on top surfaces where they'll be most vulnerable later if exposed repeatedly).

WOODWORKING

WOODWORKING

Once everything's ready then all there should really remain are these two steps which start by taking measurements from each piece including height width depth dimensions before deciding how much coverage needs & what type material thicknesses best match them respectively.

Chapter 9 - Best Interior Wood Treatments

Treatment, protection and preservation is a practise frequently associated with shielding your outdoor wood from the elements. But as a wood worker you need to know how to prevent and care about your woods. if you want to keep your floors, door and furniture strong and looking brilliant, it's important that you have the right products to hand... So what are the most essential interior treatments available?

The unique products that will save the future of your woods are oil and wax.

Both of them are necessary to protect against common household substances without cracking, flaking or peeling over time.

WOODWORKING

Treatment, protection and preservation is a practise frequently associated with shielding your outdoor wood from the elements. But as a wood worker you need to know how to prevent and care about your woods. if you want to keep your floors, door and furniture strong and looking brilliant, it's important that you have the right products to hand... So what are the most essential interior treatments available?

The unique products that will save the future of your woods are oil and wax. Both of them are necessary to protect against common household substances without cracking, flaking or peeling over time.

WOODWORKING

WOODWORKING for beginners

WOODWORKING

Oil is the best product for intensively nourishing and sealing your wood. It's also a good option if you want to give it an aged look or work on dark timber that needs more protection than wax provides... Wax,

WOODWORKING

however can be used in any room of home because there are so many different types available according as what type will suit each project - natural beeswax which has been refined with plant oils; chemical-free soybean oil based products etc) while providing some UV light resistance they're not recommended where water contact cannot occur due their porous nature compromising waterproofing properties).

Chapter 10 - How To Deal With Finishes

The most common finishes are shellac, lacquer, varnish and oil. They all have in common protection.

All are designed to inhibit the transfer of moisture and to prevent the surface from being contaminated by dirt and stains.

Shellac, lacquer and varnish are all surface finishes. This means that they do not penetrate.

Oil, on the other hand, is considered a penetrating finish because it reaches much deeper into the wood and leaves only a microscopic layer of finish on the surface. Subsequent coats continue to penetrate.

How to apply

Put some oil into the surface of the wood and begin to rub with a lint-free rag.

WOODWORKING

Allow the oil to absorb for about an hour, then wipe off the excess.

Let the surface dry for 24 hours, and then rub the whole piece with No. 0000 steel wool.

Use a tack cloth to remove all the dust before recoating.

Then apply another coat of oil as before.

For a good finish, you should apply a minimum of three coats. Once the last coat is dry and rubbed with steel wool, apply a light coat of paste wax to the entire surface. When the wax takes on a dull appearance, buff the surface to a satin sheen with a clean, dry cloth.

Step by step guide woodworking for beginners: Sharpening - Spread a layer of oil onto the surface with your fingers or use an applicator.

Allow it to soak in and penetrate into pores, then wipe off excess... - Rub lightly across any areas that need smoothing using No 000 steel wool (for final polishing). Use tack cloth before recoating if needed....

WOODWORKING

Apply layers until desired depth is reached when rubbing each coat down followed up on last application apply paste wax buff out old finish as required ... Finish product will be satin sheen without noticeable grain pattern after applying one light rubdown." The dullness should go away shortly but can also take weeks depending upon climate conditions" "This process may seem laborious at first, but it is a necessary step before the final product can be finished."

"The long-term effects of this process will make future sharpening and refinishing much easier. " (reflection) I have to admit that there was something satisfying about rubbing my new tool by hand with steel wool until its surface felt smooth for painting purposes! It has been really interesting learning how all these pieces come together in order not only finish woodworking projects; however also maintaining them as well!"

This part of the book may seem like an exhaustive list at first glance--but every single one begins from prep work or cleaning up messes made during earlier operations on your project:

WOODWORKING

-Use 100 grit sandpaper over entire length if using power tools such both circular saws and table saws. -If using hand tools, use 220 grit sandpaper over entire length.

Then: (more instructions) The first thing I did was taper the ends of my boards to make them slightly pointed on one end and then angled at a 45 degree angle with two sides touching each other . This is called tapering because it makes these edges tapered like they're going down in size from left side-to right."The second procedure required me cutting across all four board lengths so that there were three cuts made into small sections longer than what would be needed for this project--and about an inch deep as well" "I cut out strips which will later become shelves by making many crosscuts perpendicular or 90 degrees apart". Then you'll need to cut your boards to the right length (more instructions)

"Tools needed are a table saw, jointer and planer". "Jointers have edges that meet at 90 degrees from each other for accurate results. They're also used in cutting wood with an equal thickness of up by making grooves." Planers grind down one side or both sides until they match their desired height as well. (More Instructions). The tools you need may vary depending on what type project is being made so it's best not take any chances when using power equipment like circular blades which can cause injury if mishandled . Remember: Safety First!

In conclusion this step-by hand guide has been provided because most people do want some kind guidance before diving into woodworking.

Woodcraft can be a very rewarding hobby as well and one that looks great on any wall in your home or office space with the reward of seeing something you made from start to finish.

Chapter 11 - Cleaning Wood Dust

Dust is one of the hassles we, as human beings, will have to live with. Our body sheds its skin regularly by having it flake into dust, which gets on and into everything: in our homes, workspaces, even play and storage areas.

Such small amounts of dust, though, may be collected with conventional vacuum cleaners.

This is simply not the case with woodworkers, wood dust can cause serious health problems. It can cause asthma, which carpenters and joiners are four times more likely to get compared with other workers.

As they have to contend with the dust created from constantly cutting into the interlocking fibers that are the main structural component of wood. This means that sheds, shops and many other areas used by woodworkers will often be filled with amounts of dust too large for a conventional vacuum cleaner to handle. This is where they turn to heavy duty dust collection systems to do the job.

A heavy duty dust collection system will be able to filter the air and capture most of it, which is then ejected into a separate container. This can also help prolong equipment life as well - without regular maintenance from these systems there are higher chances that motors or other electrical components could become clogged with wood particles in time meaning they must eventually replaced altogether."

- clean up any sawdust left on surfaces before leaving your work area (this includes tables) for safety reasons; make sure you wear gloves when doing this because some cuttings have sharp edges!

It's important not only keep yourself safe but others who may visit later so ensure after cleaning all areas used by using disposable cloths/paper towels

and dispose of them in a sealed container to avoid spillage or contact with any chemicals.

WOODWORKING

"When you are done, put your tools away and clean up the area where you were working." - this includes sweeping floors/dusting furniture around work space if needed! If after finishing for day make sure store all equipment properly such as sharp objects into case & cover table top so it doesn't get scratched by other items; unplug power cords from outlets before leaving shop (this will help prevent accidental electric shocks)

These safety measures should always be practiced when doing woodworking projects because accidents may happen which could cause injury- sometimes not only just temporary injuries but even life threatening ones too!"

Chapter 12 - Working safely

Woodworking is among one of the safest and enjoyable hobbies you can do, but you need to follow simple and easy rules for your own safety.

The work shop is not the place to careless. It is the place to learn and adopt good safety working habits which will in turn make woodworking more fun and enjoyable.

1. Always Wear Safety Equipment

Wear ear protection during usage of loud power tools like routers and surface planers and latex gloves while applying finishes. NEVER BE WITHOUT YOUR SAFETY **GLASSES**. These should be the first thing you reach for when entering the shop. When you're buying a pair of safety **gloves**, you're looking for secure grip and a good sense of feel through the fingers so you know you're handling materials and products safely. You want thick, abrasion-resistant material on the palms and fingers as these are the parts of your hands that will be coming into regular contact with sharp edges, blades, and rough surfaces.

If gloves are very important , **earplugs** and **dust mask** are no less important.

WOODWORKING

WOODWORKING for beginners

2. Wear The Right Clothes

Try to always wear clothes that protect you for the woodworking environment, Also always remove any metal or dangling jewellery.

3. Avoid Using Anything That Can Impair Your Reaction Time and Judgement

You want to stay out of the alcohol and drug cabinets to avoid injuries.

When wood working, the dangers can be even higher by inadvertently using the wrong tool.

4. Disconnect Power

Always remember to disconnect the power source itself before changing blades or bits on your power tools.

5. Never Use Blunt Blades & Bits

While this might seem obvious seeing as how dangerous a dull cutting tool can be. Dull tools will need to be made to work harder to cut and as a result can bind or kick back. Sharp bits and blades will ensure cleaner cuts as well.

6. Never Reach Over A Running Blade

Always wait until a spinning blade has stopped moving before reaching to remove waste or cut-offs etc.

Chapter 13 - First Aid Kit for Woodworkers

Woodworking is an art and a hobby that many people enjoy. However, it can be very difficult to know where you should begin when trying woodwork for the first time-- especially if this will not always have much experience with tools or home repair projects! The following chapter offers some great advice about how beginners in particular might get started on their own project without any problems whatsoever:

WOODWORKING

I want to be fair regarding this topic and I hope you appreciate my honesty. Woodworkers spend a lifetime handling razor-sharp tools, power equipment with exposed blades, and boards that harbor splinters and fasteners. The more you will get familiar to this familiar to this world the more you will know what I mean about that. In this environment, there's always the risk of an injury. Usually woodworkers cut their fingers, and occasionally the palms of their hands. Although the hand often will recover from minor injuries even if it receives no care at all, recovery is faster with less scarring and less risk of infection if it's treated properly. For more serious cuts and eye injuries, however, what you do first can have an impact on the rest of your life.

Let me tell you to forget the first-aid kits offered in drug stores. Forget much of the misguided advice found in popular manuals. The woodworking environment is unique, and I'll tell you about some specialized equipment and supplies that work well there.

WOODWORKING

The woodworking environment is unique, and I'll tell you about some specialized equipment and supplies that work well there. I'll also show you a few tricks on treating

wounds—from stopping bleeding to cleaning to bandaging—based on proven

medical principles. In the end, you'll learn how to treat injuries in a way that

gets you back to work as soon as possible.

A first-aid kit for woodworkers looks very different from the kits

sold in drugstores. It contains materials for closing cuts, flexible

coverings for wounds, tools for removing splinters, and eye wash.

Many of these products are available from

multiple manufacturers.

1. Coban tape

2. Glue syringe

3. Eye wash

4. Tegaderm bandages

5. Band-Aids

6. Examination gloves

7. Magnifying lens

8. Steri-Strips

9. X-Acto knife

10. Krazy Glue

11. Scissors

12. Tape

13. Tweezers

Chapter 14 - How To Handle Most Cuts

1. Soap and water

The most effective treatment for all wounds is immediate washing with soap and clean water. (You can skip this if you need to go to the emergency room, because they will clean it there). Washing drastically reduces the number of germs, and takes away dirt and debris in which bacteria can hide and multiply.

2. Five minutes of pressure

After washing the wound, you need to stop the bleeding. Apply pressure directly over the wound for five minutes without interruption to help form a clot. If you peek, the clock starts all over again.

3. Close the wound before bandaging

When you get cut, keeping the two edges of the wound firmly closed will help it heal rapidly.

WOODWORKING

EYES

Rinse carefully or see a doctor. When you cut wood, especially with a router or table saw, sawdust (and sometimes other material) will fly. If some of that small debris ends up in your eye, your natural tears will usually wash it away. If the debris digs in and resists being washed away by tears, the best answer is to retract the eyelid away from the eyeball, and flush the eye with an eye-wash solution. Get someone to help you.

Woodworking is a hobby that can be done at home, or in the garage. It's also an excellent way to create personalized gifts for friends and family members on special occasions. No matter what your skill level may be, you'll find some wood project ideas here!

Chapter 15 - DIY Projects: Stowaway Bench

Recommended dimensions:

Dimensions 1: L: 68 cm, W: 35 cm, H: 45 cm

Dimensions 2: L: 111 cm, W: 35 cm, H: 45 cm

Material: Plywood, hardwood

The tools and materials you need for this project are :

Timber, all timber requirements can be cut for you at any warehouse by the team members in timber

18 volt drill

20 up to 30 mil screws

Tape measure

WOODWORKING

Good industrial PVR,

Clamps

A hammer

A pencil

Sandpaper

Satin Polyurethane Finish

The first step is to prepare the base, the sit of the box so once you have chosen your dimensions take the one for the base and glue and screw the piece of pine at the base of each side. That's where the floor is going to sit.

We now are going to attach the base to the two sides and that's simply by gluing and just tacking with some, some breads.

Once we finish this side, you just repeat on the other side.

WOODWORKING

Now that we have the base together, all we will do is glue and screw on the front piece of wood and then on the back.

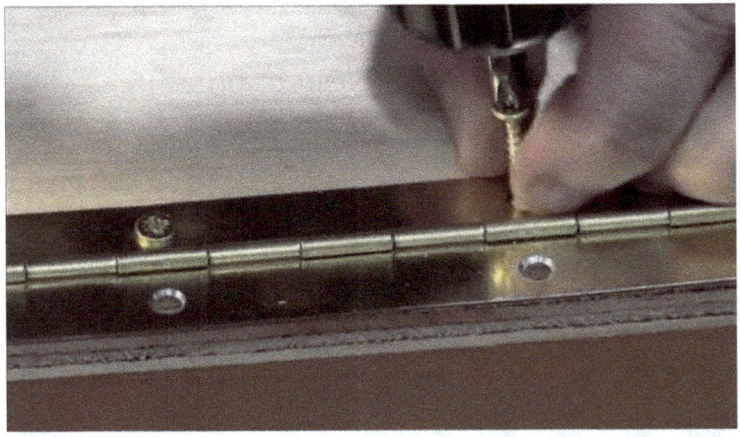

Now we've got two sides on the back and the front. We're now going to put the lid on and by using a piano hinge, you are going to attach this by screwing it to the top of the lid.

Make sure to put all the screws in because the lid has got a lot of weight and then we're going to screw on the other side of the hinge to top of box. There we go, nice big storage box with blankets and whatever you can think of.

WOODWORKING

You can personalize this any way you like. You can finish it or not, it depends how you like it if you do, if you do make sure to use sandpaper and some satin polyurethane finish.

Here below find the care directions.

Care:

Step 1:
Clean the surface with a mild soapy water solution. Wipe the surface dry to remove any excess soap that may have been left behind and start from a fresh, clean slate.

Step 2:
Apply a furniture oil with a clean cloth for two minutes. Excess oil must be removed in 30 minutes after application.

Step 3:
Wax the surface with a clean cloth until an even shine is attained. The oil will not harden for 12 hours; do not cover it until then.

DIY Projects - Wine Box

Tools you will need:

Hammer, Tape measure, Framing square, Level

Miter saw, Drill machinery, Screwdriver, Sander

Post hole digger, Concrete mixer

Materials list:

- A – 2 pieces of 3/8" wood – 2 1/2"x4 1/4" long, 2 pieces – 2 1/2"x13 1/2" long **BOX**
- B – 1 piece of 3/8" wood – 4 1/4"x13 1/2" **long BOTTOM**
- C – 2 pieces of 3/8" wood – 1 1/4"x4 1/4" long, 2 pieces – 1 1/4"x13 1/2" **long LID**
- D – 1 piece of 3/8" wood – 4 1/4"x13 1/2" **long TOP**

Step 1

Build the frame for the wine box. You can use 3/8" wood, plywood or even 1x3s. Cut both sides of the slats at 45 degrees to make miter joints. Add glue, align the edges and use brad nails to lock the components together.

Step 2

Cut and attach the bottom part to the frame of the box. Align the edges and make sure they are flush.

Add glue to the joints and insert brad nails.

Step 3

Build the top lid from 3/8" wood. Adjust the with to 1 1/4". Cut both sides of the components at 45 degrees. Make sure the corners are square and align the edges with attention. Add glue to the joints and insert brad nails.

Step 4

Attach the top of the frame. Align the edges, making sure they are flush. Use brad nails and glue to lock the top to the frame of the lid.

Use small hinges to secure the lid to the wine box.

Add a latch to the front of the wine box. This detail will enhance the look of the project and make it look more authentic.

WOODWORKING

DIY Projects - Candle Holder

Material

Find boards of soft woods, pine is perfect. If old and to throw away they are still good to be used.

Use Bevel gauge for measuring.

Steps:

Take the bevel gauge and set the angle at 14 degrees.

The length of the dovetails on each board will equal the thickness of one end board. Each dovetail should be exactly 5/8". To make sure that's true, mark a "stop" line on your first board at 5/8", then make another stop line 5/8" from the other end.

Use only two dovetails per corner. Measure in 1/4" from the edge of the board and angle down to the stopped line. Then measure 3/8" along either of these lines, finishing by angling back to the end of the board.

To make life a little bit easier, you can shade the area that you want to cut out. It is helpful to avoid any confusion during the process of cutting out lines.

In order to make a candle box, take the scroll saw and begin creating.

Cut on the inside of all your notches to make uniform holes. Then cut out that line across one box and one line across your other box. This should be completed on both boxes or else everything would fall apart as you put them together.

After cutting out the parts, use a pencil or whiteout to trace the silhouette of the parts on each end of each board.

After cutting out the pieces, align one end piece with an adjoining side piece so there is equal spacing between them. Repeat this with remaining boards.

Working only with the end pieces now, draw another "stop" line on the top and bottom of the end board. Next you will draw lines from the profile of the dovetails down to the stop lines.

Do this on both sides of the board. Repeat this process for each end of the end boards.

When you have all of your reference lines drawn on the end pieces, go ahead and shade in the areas to be cut out. If using a scroll saw, tilt the table to 14 degrees to make the cuts.

When following the lines cut on the waste side of the line.

To remove the waste wood from your "stop" line, you can easily use a chisel and mallet. If you try it with a scroll saw, you have to reset the table to zero degrees and take out a portion of the waste wood and chisel out the remainder.

Put the side and end piece together and see where the restrictions are that won't allow the joint to go together.

Remove very small portions of wood with a chisel or knife. Test often until the two pieces go together perfectly. If you see some gaps in your joint these will be filled with wood putty.

Working with one corner at a time, coat the sides of each dovetail and areas where the pieces of wood touch each other with a thin coat of glue. Dovetails are a very strong joints by themselves and don't require too much to hold them together.

Be careful not to get so much glue that it squeezes out and becomes a problem to remove later. The glue that gets on the surface will cause an unsightly appearance when you put the finishing touches on your box if not removed or sanded off.

With all of the corners assembled with glue, take a square to make sure your box will set up nice and square. Let glue dry.

It is time to cut the bottom to fit your box. With this box I had some pieces of good quality finished plywood that was 1/2" thick.

measure the opening of your box bottom. Select your material that you are using and cut it to size. I always to prefer cutting a bottom just slightly too large and using a sander,

Adding the slide track for the lid.

WOODWORKING

The next step is to make the pieces that will enable the lid to slide to open and close. I start with pieces that are at least 2" wide. I do this so that I can keep my fingers well away from the saw blade.

I cut a square notch out of the corner of the board that is 3/8" x 3/8" to accommodate the lid. Then I will rip the 2" down to 3/4".

After making the pieces, miter the ends with a 45 degree cut. Dry fit everything to make sure it looks good. If it does, then glue the pieces on with a light coat of glue only where the pieces touch the rest of the box. If the fit is close and not perfect, sandpaper will take care of the details after the glue dries.

Pieces only go on the sides and one end. The other end allows the lid to move in and out.

When the glue dries, take off the clamps and then sand all of the joints smooth. I like to use an orbital sander with 120 grit paper for this. It will flatten everything out and smooth the surface nicely.

Making the lid.

With your slide track mounted on your box, take a careful measurement from the recessed part of the track on both sides. Take another measurement from the recessed part of the track from end to the edge. This will be your lid dimension.

Once your board is cut to size, it's time to put a bevel on it on three sides. This gives the lid a raised panel look. On my particular board, it was 6 1/8" wide and using a test piece first, I determined that an 18 degree angle would give me the look that I was after.

You can put on any kind of finish that you desire here.

Chapter 16 - Build Your Own Garage Workbench

A garage workbench is an essential piece of equipment in any home workshop. A workbench will allow you to complete projects easily and with greater accuracy. A variety of pre made workbenches are available to fit your needs. If you prefer, you can make your own workbench, either with a kit or from a plan.

Choosing a garage workbench

Workbenches are available in a wide variety of sizes and styles. Benches are great for woodworking, crafts and other household projects. You can purchase a bench at most home improvement stores. Another option is to build your own bench. You can find plans in books and on the internet with instructions to create the perfect bench to suit your needs.

A table style workbench is made of heavy duty materials to stand up to regular use. Most models have a hardwood top with metal legs. Table tops can also be made of steel. These resemble a typical table shape with nothing underneath.

Cabinet style benches have drawers or cabinets in the space under the table top. This is great for utilizing otherwise wasted space. This method allows for additional storage space. Some have a pegboard backing that is perfect for hanging hand tools. You won't need to dig through drawers or a tool box to find what you need.

A power strip bench is a good choice if you use power tools often. These come with up to nine outlets in a strip with a heavy duty power cord. They also have current protection to prevent overload. These can be either six or eight foot benches. Some have a tool caddy to hold smaller tools.

Build Your Own Workbench

WOODWORKING

Consider building your own bench to get exactly what you want. Kits are available with everything you need to create your bench. Instructions and materials are included with the kit. With this method, you will be limited to the kit's design. The benefit is that all pieces are pre cut. You won't need to worry about uneven cuts.

You can build your own bench and purchase all the materials. This method is a bit more complicated, but you have more control about the final outcome. Free workbench plans are available on the internet with detailed instructions for you to follow. Cut the plywood according to the directions and be sure to make your cuts straight.

For best results, choose good quality wood, oak or a hardwood plywood is an excellent choice. Use several coats of polyurethane to protect the top of the bench. Be sure to sand between each coat. A good urethane coating makes messes easier to clean up when working on projects later.

Organizing and Making Room in your Garage

You will need to organize your garage and create storage space to make room for workbenches. Determine what you need to store. Start with a good clean out and get rid of things you don't need. Throw away old paint and other junk. Give away or donate old items, tools or other things that are too good to throw away, but that you don't need any more.

The walls of your garage offer great opportunities for storage space. Cabinets are great for organizing clutter. High cabinets are good for storing chemicals and paints. Sharp items can be put up high to keep them away from children. Consider locks if you have young children. Locker cabinets are perfect for larger items. Drawers are good for organizing tools, fishing equipment and other small items.

Chapter 17 - A Guide To Woodworking Plans

Woodworking plans are an essential component of any project. Wood working patterns and scroll saw patterns are needed to plan a project and create accents in your piece. Good plans give step by step instructions, diagrams and illustrations to guide you through from start to finish. You can buy plans, find them for free on the internet or make your own plan.

Finding Woodworking Plans

Free woodworking patterns can be found on the internet. Many are free, but others need to be purchased. You can search for general plans or for specific projects. Patterns are available for everything from a simple box or bird feeder to elaborate furniture projects. Several websites offer plans for making children's toys and decorative items. Enter the project you are looking for in your favourite search engine or just enter free woodworking plans.

WOODWORKING

There are books available that are devoted to wood working patterns. You can find these at book stores, on the internet or in your local library. Often, woodworking magazines will contain plans for a wide variety of projects. Purchase a few of these at your local news stand. After you have found one you like best, you may decide to subscribe and receive new plans month after month.

If you are new to woodworking, it's best to start of with a simple pattern. This will help you learn to read and follow the plans. As your skills increase, you can move on to more difficult projects. Start off with a simple toy or bird feeder before attempting to make a dining room set. Look for detailed and thorough plans to help you create your project.

Good plans include detailed instructions. The instructions should take you step by step through the entire project. Look for plans that have detailed diagrams as well as illustrations of the project at each stage. Print out your plans and keep them in a binder. This will help keep you organized and prevent pages from getting lost or damaged.

WOODWORKING

You can follow the plan step by step or you may decide to make a few changes to the plan. Changing a few details is a great way to make a generic plan more personal and original. For example, you can change certain designs or accent pieces and give the project a whole new look. Another option is to paint the finished product, rather than staining.

Creating Woodworking Plans

Once you become more experienced, you may decide to try to create your own plan. Start by sketching how you want the finished product to look. The first sketch doesn't need to be too technical or detailed. You will add the details and dimensions later. Once you have made your original sketch, determine the dimensions of the total finished product.

Determine what type of wood you will use in your project and how much wood you will need. It's important to use accurate measurements when ordering the wood to avoid running out before the project is finished. Determine what other materials you will need to complete the project. This will help you estimate the total cost.

WOODWORKING

Create a detailed list of all materials needed and the quantity of each material. Include items such as paint, stain or polyurethane. Consider the tools that will be needed to complete the project. Do you have all that you need? With this information, you can then determine the overall cost. Take this list with you when you go out to purchase supplies.

You will then draw a more detailed sketch of your design. Create diagrams like those found in woodworking plans on the internet. Draw each stage of the process in detail. Write out detailed instructions that will take you step by step through the project. This will help you stay organized and ensure that you don't skip any essential steps along the way.

Chapter 18 - Classic Furniture A Timeless Style

But among the many ways to decorate, the classic style is certainly one who most reflects the true nature of full furniture landscape, the wide range of furniture and its variants are in fact a landmark in the production of any furniture factory.

The classic style impose itself in the proposed furniture to be timeless, adaptable to any environment, presents enviable modularity and functionality that join the preciousness of lines and materials will creating an evocative harmony.

The new design studies now have developed new designs for classics furniture from the old flavor but approach with maximum functionality in everyday life.

The classic style is characterized by its very nature by a wide use of wood, especially furniture are cherry-wood and oak, as well as mahogany and solid wood; recall the Old and warmth's wood are the fundamental characteristic of this style. This style is revisited today by artisanal production that makes it accessible even in contemporary environments while maintaining the value and flavor that only with an accurate woodworking can have.

The classic furniture is timeless and fills the environment with his compactness, does relive the warmth of a time and at the same time is a sign of prestige and sophistication. The craftsmanship embellish every detail so that there are showcases and beliefs from golden profiles well matching with shelves in marble and granite.

The furniture direct on the craft and their validity for this are well known for furniture production by finishing sought such coatings and drawings by hand worked well using over colors and lacquerings. The elegance and the study of detail often makes the difference and processing carried out by experienced operators often leads to have a piece of furniture that not only is never equal to another. In the decorations made by hand, the quest for lines and soft colors, wants to rediscover the ancient and valuable of technical master craftsmen of the past.

The processing and use of wood is the quality that makes the difference and a good production is in furniture that have "life" and giving "life" that decorate the environment. Thus the classic furniture, maintains his desire to ancient but lives in the life of today where required functionality and practicality. In classic style is a beautiful harmonic fusion between ancient's scent and the modern 's comfort.

Darren J. Brann is a master craftsman and furniture maker, who began his woodworking hobby in the mid-seventies. Eventually, Darren's affection evolved into a love affair of sorts with furniture making, and he began to build full time in northwestern Connecticut. Now retired from his trade, Darren gets to enjoy his workshop most every day.

www.ingramcontent.com/pod-product-compliance
Lightning Source LLC
Chambersburg PA
CBHW051705160426
43209CB00004B/1034